The Boy
and the
Biggest Statue

Written and Illustrated by Mizanur Rahman

First written in 2007 and first published in paperback in 2010 by Happy Books.

Text and illustrations written and owned by Mohammed Mizanur Rahman. Any part of this publication, including text and illustrations may be reproduced, stored and transmitted by any means, electronic, mechanical, photocopying, recording or otherwise without prior permission of the owner or publisher provided they are always attributed to the original owner mentioned here and not misrepresented, distorted, misquoted or attributed to any other author.

Visit our website: www.happy-books.co.uk

ISBN 978-1-907622-07-6

For my daughter Sumayyah and all other Muslim children

The Boy and the Biggest Statue

Now listen carefully
to what I am going to do.
I am going to tell you
a story that is true,
about an honest person,
just like you,
and a very big statue.

This is a story about a boy.
He was young and full of joy.
He lived in a time,
long long ago,
when everything
moved quite slow.
There were no cars,
phones or chocolate bars,
no TV and no popstars.

Instead, people had time to think.
They had to fetch their own
water to drink
and they used to go
outside to play,
but always made time to pray.
The boy's name was Ibraheem.
He was very polite
and always kept clean.
Just like you,
he had a mummy and a daddy
that he always listened to.
He loved them a lot
and he never forgot
how they looked after him
when he was just a tot.
Ibraheem was a very clever boy
that never lied

and he always tried,
the very best he could,
to always be good.
He was glad
for everything he had:
his home, friends
and his mum and dad.

Ibraheem couldn't
wait to grow up,
so that, as soon as he was ready,
he could get married too
and be a daddy.

Everybody liked Ibraheem
because he told others
to be good
and not to be naughty;
whether they were young
or even if they were forty!

As Ibraheem got older
he also got bolder.
He always was very clever
and that's why he never
copied those who were bad,
although some naughty
people wished that he had.

Ibraheem saw his father
and his friends one day
going off to pray.
They went to a statue
that they always used to talk to.
Ibraheem thought this was silly.
He knew that statues
didn't talk really.
He always wondered why people
worshipped those statues
when they cannot talk or move
and he didn't have a clue
what people expected
the statues to do!

In his town,
people worshipped many things.
Some prayed to the sun
or the moon
and others worshipped statues.
They used to bow down
and even give them food!
Whether they offered
fruit or meat,
Ibraheem knew
they couldn't eat.

Ibraheem was confused.
He knew there was a God,
or else, where did
everything come from?
But he found what
everyone was doing very strange
and he thought
it was time for a change.

One night, he looked up at a star.
It was very bright,
even from so far.
He wondered if it was possible
that this was the Lord
that everybody adored.
But when it set
and vanished from view,
he realised that it cannot be God

Then he looked at the moon
as it rose out of the gloom.
It was round,
bright and very proud.
Ibraheem thought,
"Maybe this is my Lord …"
But then it set and vanished too.
So he knew
that it simply couldn't be true.

God is neither
the star nor the moon,
he said,

"If my Lord
doesn't help me soon.
I will be lost
and won't know what to do."

In the morning,
Ibraheem was up early,
while the dew
was still clear and pearly.
He saw the sun rise
like a cheerful surprise,
bright in the sky.

Ibraheem called,
"Maybe this is my Lord!
It is much bigger after all!"
But the sun too,
set and disappeared
just as Ibraheem had feared.

So he realised.
The stories were all lies.
The sun and the moon
didn't deserve to be worshipped,
because after they had risen,
they would always set and hide.
They come and go like people do
and they cannot hear us,
even if they try to.
He also thought about the statues.
How can they help us
when even the sun couldn't do?

We should only pray
to the Lord
that made us all:
The One who made the stars,
the moon, the sun
and the earth too.
We shouldn't pray
to an idol instead of the Lord,
nor pretend
that it is God
or even His friend.

So Ibraheem went out
and told the people.
But they were naughty
and wouldn't listen.
They were already smitten.
They didn't want
to leave their idols.
Ibraheem asked his father,

"Why do you bother?
Worshipping things
that cannot help you
or even hurt you!
How can God be a simple statue
that was itself built by you
with your own two hands?"

But his father didn't understand. Ibraheem yearned for Allah to help his father learn and to forgive him for his sins.

Ibraheem told everyone,
but they wouldn't listen
and kept making fun.
But Ibraheem had an idea.
He would wait
until nobody was near,
when they were too far
to see him or hear.

Then he would show them all
how silly they'd been.
He went to all the statues
and made sure
he hadn't been seen.

Then he took a hammer
and broke them all
except the biggest one.
Then he left the hammer on it
when he was done.

When the people came back
they saw the terrible mess.
"Who has broken our idols?"
They tried to guess.
"We heard a young boy
talk about them, making jest!
His name was Ibraheem."
They had guessed.

They said,
"Bring him forward
so he can confess."
They brought Ibraheem
and asked,
"Was it you, Ibraheem?
Who broke our gods
made of clay,
while we were all away?"

Ibraheem wanted them
to think about what they say.
How can God
be made out of clay?
How can the Lord
so easily break
with just a little shake?

So Ibraheem told them this,
"Maybe the big one did it!
Why not ask him
if you think he can speak?"

But they all knew
that statues couldn't talk.
In fact, they would surely have
escaped if only they could walk!

Angry with Ibraheem
they wanted him
punished and blamed.
They said "We should
burn him in flames!"

So they built a huge fire
that grew
higher and higher.
It was so big
that they couldn't put
Ibraheem in!
So they built a catapult
that could throw
and they brought everyone
out to see the show.

They threw Ibraheem
through the air
with the wind in his hair.

But before he fell into the heat,
wondering
if he would land on his feet,
just in the nick of time,
the true Lord,
who had been watching
all the while,
said,

"O fire!
Be cool and peace
for Ibraheem."

So instead of smoke and steam,
Ibraheem
enjoyed his stay in the fire,
which still grew
higher and higher,

as if he were on
holiday at the beach
with the ocean within his reach.
He had the time of his life
because he had been wise,
while the people
couldn't believe their eyes!

Years later,
Ibraheem had got on
with his life.
Just as he had dreamed,
he now had a wife.
He was also a dad,
two sons he had!

But he was worried that his boys
might take statues as toys.
So he prayed to the Lord
to save him and his boys
from the idols that he deplored.

Ibraheem and his sons
built a house for Allah
called the Ka'bah
that people face from afar
whenever they pray,
even till today.

So Allah saved all three
and all three were prophets.
So they would never
pray to any idol ever!
They would always be clever
and one day,
would go to heaven forever.

THE END

Notes & References

This story about the prophet Ibraheem (peace be upon him) has been adapted for children and is not taken directly from the Qur'an, though it is based on Qur'anic verses.

For more accurate elaborations of this story, you can refer to the following verses of the Qur'an:

- Chapter no.6 of the Qur'an "Surah al An'aam", verses 74-83
- Chapter no.19 of the Qur'an "Surah al Maryam", verses 46-50
- Chapter no.26 of the Qur'an "Surah al Shu'araa", verses 69-87
- Chapter no.37 of the Qur'an "Surah al Saffaat", verses 83-100
- Chapter no.21 of the Qur'an "Surah al Anbiyaa", verses 51-71
- Chapter no.14 of the Qur'an "Surah Ibraheem", verses 35

Parts of this story may also be found in many Ahadeeth (narrations) of the prophet Muhammad (saw) and Tafaaseer (Commentaries) of the Qur'an.

Further Reading

Other details of the life of Ibraheem (peace be upon him) can be found in the following chapters of the Qur'an:

- Chapter no.2 of the Qur'an "Surah al Baqarah", verses 124-127, 130-136 and 258-260
- Chapter no.4 of the Qur'an "Surah al Nisaa", verses 54 and 125
- Chapter no.9 of the Qur'an "Surah al Tawbah", verses 113-114
- Chapter no.11 of the Qur'an "Surah Hud", verses 69-76
- Chapter no.14 of the Qur'an "Surah Ibraheem", verses 35-52
- Chapter no.15 of the Qur'an "Surah al Hijr", verses 51-60
- Chapter no.16 of the Qur'an "Surah al Nahl", verses 120-123
- Chapter no.29 of the Qur'an "Surah al 'Ankaboot", verses 16-19 and 31-32
- Chapter no.37 of the Qur'an "Surah al Saffaat", verses 83-113
- Chapter no.43 of the Qur'an "Surah al Zukhruf", verses 26-29
- Chapter no.51 of the Qur'an "Surah al Dhaariyaat", verses 24-33
- Chapter no.60 of the Qur'an "Surah al Mumtahinah", verses 4-6

And many other verses of the Qur'an …

The Ka'bah today is the Qiblah of all Muslims around the world. Muslims face the direction of the Ka'bah in Makkah whenever they pray to Allah.

The gates of the Ka'bah nowadays is decorated and the entire house is covered with black cloth.

Millions of Muslims from around the world travel to Makkah every year to worship at the Masjid built by Ibraheem.

Other titles available from

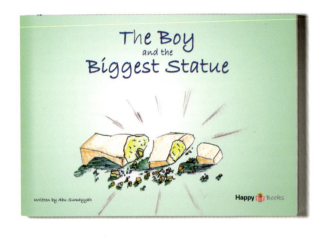

The Boy and the Biggest Statue

The story of the Prophet Ibraheem (peace be upon him) as a child exploring the world around him and discovering his true Lord and his struggle with his people to discourage Shirk (polytheism).

RRP £5.00

Other titles available from

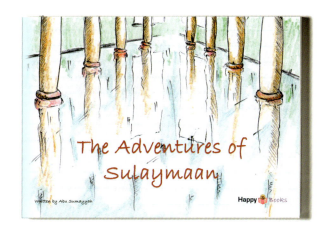

The Adventures of Sulaymaan

The story of the Prophet Sulaymaan (peace be upon him) and his special gifts from Allah such as the ability to speak to animals and how he used them to rule in justice and invite Bilqees to Islam.

RRP £5.00

Other titles available from

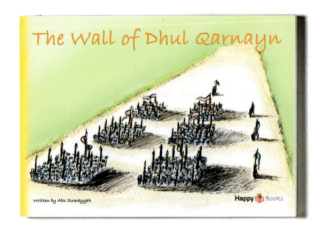

The Wall of Dhul Qarnayn

The story of Dhul Qarnayn, a just ruler with full authority in the earth and how he tackles the giant monster-like Ya'jooj and Ma'jooj tribes.

RRP £5.00

Other titles coming soon from

Dawood and the Giant
The Adventures of Musa (Part 1)
The Adventures of Musa (Part 2)
The Adventures of Musa (Part 3)
Maryam's Miracle

and many more inshaa Allah ...